Goddess Aphasia

A Stroke Survivor and His Dual Muse

SHAI ANBAR

Goddess Aphasia
A Stroke Survivor and His Dual Muse
Copyright © 2022 Shai Anbar

Produced and printed by Stillwater River Publications.
All rights reserved. Written and produced in the
United States of America. This book may not be reproduced
or sold in any form without the expressed, written
permission of the author and publisher.

Visit our website at
www.StillwaterPress.com
for more information.

First Stillwater River Publications Edition

ISBN: 978-1-958217-39-9

1 2 3 4 5 6 7 8 9 10
Written by Shai Anbar
Cover & interior book design by Matthew St. Jean
Published by Stillwater River Publications,
Pawtucket, RI, USA

The views and opinions expressed
in this book are solely those of the author
and do not necessarily reflect the views
and opinions of the publisher.

To Ana and Isaac

Contents

A Man and His Pain ix
Prologue xi

Part I: The Man I Used to Be
    The Calm Before My Storm....................... 1
    Write On 5
    What Planet Did You Come From? 9
    In Purgatory 21
    Routine 25
    Flunked Out... 32

Part II: My Private War
    Pet Peeve.. 39
    Charred Memories................................... 43
    The Trauma Club 49
    My Winter of Discontent 52
    A Change of Heart...................................55

Part III: The Light Within
    Our Own Tree Story............................... 61
    Aphasia, Meet Mom 64
    Yogi for Hire 70
    All Together Now 74
    Fare Thee Well... 77
    Afterword 85

Acknowledgements..*87*
About the Author..*89*

GODDESS APHASIA

A Man and His Pain

A man and his pain:
one embraces the other,
cut from the same cloth.
Between twilights and dawns,
loves and torments,
down a narrow path they march,
a man and his pain.

Rainy seasons follow their same loneliness;
days of scorching heat follow their shadows'
namelessness.
Just like Pyramus and Thisbe,
in their lives
and in their deaths,
they make their own way:
a man and his pain.

And there's no room for questions
or redundant mercy—
only for acceptance
of the ancient covenant.
When lovers fall on their swords,
splashing blood on white mulberry fruits
turning them dark,
so does a man and his pain.

Prologue

You know what aphasia is? If not, then pull up a chair and hear me out.

Aphasia is a communication disorder that affects over two million Americans, resulting from damage to areas of the brain that produce and process language. A person with aphasia can have trouble speaking, reading, writing, and—especially in my case—comprehending. Even formulating inner speech—the silent expression of conscious thought to oneself in a coherent linguistic form—is challenging. Impairment of these abilities can range from mild to very severe; mine is the former. Some of us have difficulty in only one aspect of communication, such as putting words into meaningful sentences or understanding what others are saying. More commonly, people who have aphasia—I'll call us "aphasians"—are limited in more than one area. Nearly all aphasians have difficulty finding words—names of people, places, things, or events—and some, like mistakenly substitute words with similar-sounding ones, accidentally transposing the initial sounds or letters of two or more words, often to a humorous effect.

Hun, did you wake Snoopy for a talk?

Most people have never heard of aphasia, which I find interesting because most people know about strokes. What causes aphasia? It frequently stems from a stroke. Currently, there are nearly 7 million stroke survivors in the U.S., and about 795,000 people suffer a stroke each year. There are at least 2 million people who have aphasia and nearly 180,000 Americans acquire it each year. So, do the math: about a third, or 33%, of people who suffer from a stroke will develop aphasia.

Each person's experience with aphasia is unique, from the extent of the damage to the location of the stroke or brain injury to one's age, general health, and ability to recover. Me? Almost ten years ago, at the age of fifty-one, I had a stroke—an ischemic one. You know, "the sudden loss of blood circulation to an area of the brain, resulting in a corresponding loss of neurologic function .. etc." Physically speaking, my health turned out fine and dandy. Well, kinda; age is a bitch sometimes, as my newfound arthritis will tell you. The blood thinners and cholesterol-lowering drugs don't help either. But it's my mental and spiritual recovery that is, was, and always will be an ongoing, turtle-paced journey.

Hm, "recovery" … I prefer "*dis*covery." But let me put that on hold for now.

The main treatment for aphasia is speech therapy, which is "the assessment and treatment of communication problems and speech disorders. Individually or in groups, patients are led by speech-language pathologists (SLPs), often referred to as speech therapists." Aphasians relearn and practice language skills, sometimes finding other ways to communicate. Family members and caregivers participate in the process, and friends—true ones—often have our back. All these things give us comfort, strength, and hope for better days, because too frequently our skies are gray and cloudy.

Aphasia stripped away my joy, my pride, and my dignity. Aphasia was responsible for my loss of language and friends, both of which I dearly loved as well as ruining my successful career. My broken dreams and vanished years all rolled into one, tucked under the tattered umbrella that spelled "disability."

That is, until I was shown the light in the strangest of places—because I finally looked at it right.

How so, you ask? Because an uninvited guest came into my miserable life, took me by the hand and transformed me into the man I am today.

Folks, meet Aphasia.

Confused?

Don't worry. You won't be.

PART I

The Man I Used to Be

1

The Calm Before My Storm

Here's a bio of mine that was circulated online by an international software technology startup in the fall of 2011.

Our President and CEO, Shai Anbar, leads the operational, technical, sales and marketing efforts in the Americas, driving strategic planning, execution, and global operations. Shai has over twenty years' experience in the logistics and security industry, focusing on key growth initiatives. His diverse background ranges from established companies to fledgling secure tech startups to compliance and process data management software. Prior to joining our management team, Shai spent seventeen years with Brink's Global Services, which spans over 100 countries and specializes in diamonds, jewelry, precious metals, currency, technology and other valuables. Being in charge of 400+

employees, Shai played an instrumental role in the setup and development of startup operations around the world, and has launched new business lines in the secure logistics and information protection arenas. Prior to that, Shai founded New Mile, a firm specializing in financial advisory and consulting services, which includes M&A and strategic investments that cater to unique, entrepreneurial startups.

Shai earned a B.A. from Rutgers-Camden University in New Jersey and a Master's in Philosophy from Temple University in Philadelphia, Pennsylvania.

The job had one minor caveat: the company's headquarters were located north of Boston. When I was hired, I treated myself by leasing a second hand, low mileage, no-frills BMW 328i. I named her Bertha, my queen of the road, and settled in for the 230-mile schlep from my family home in Montclair, NJ to Boston. For four months I drove four hours on Sunday nights, and then back again on Friday nights just in time for the weekend.

That weekend I didn't have to travel. I had to get a minor procedure, simple enough, something called ablation—correcting an uneven heart rhythm known as arrhythmia. The next day I'd be back on the road and talking business. I'd already had my first ablation a couple of years earlier—a failure, but why not give it a second chance? Mind you, my arrhythmia was manageable; my heartbeat wasn't too fast or too slow, just … irregular. But it was bothersome because it made me feel tired.

On that fateful day, December 6, 2011, I woke up at 5 a.m. and jumped straight on my treadmill in my basement. A shit, shave, and shower later, I turned Bertha's engine on and headed out to Valley Hospital in Ridgewood. I got the royal treatment: a comfy bed; a flowery gown; a nurse wearing an angelic smile, prepping and then escorting me to the operating room. The anesthesiologist's needle put me into a deep, tranquil sleep.

When I opened my eyes, I could feel something was wrong. I was supposed to be resting at the Recovery Room—I'd titled it "The VIP Lounge" after my first ablation—dusting away the cobwebs of sedation. Instead of sipping black coffee from a Styrofoam cup and munching on Oreos, I was being wheeled hurriedly on a stretcher by three or four nurses, my wife close behind. My eyes hopelessly followed the fluorescent lights moving past on the corridor's ceiling. Then came an elevator; the doors closed and up we went.

I rose slightly, turning my head towards my wife. It was time for me to ask what the hell was happening.

"Lamadawa, lo ke ni …"

I stopped talking. I froze. I was scared. What the hell was I saying?

I tried again. "Eh, de, ani … la za …"

"Shhhh, it's okay, Shai," she said, to calm me down. "You had a stroke."

Ding! Ding!

The elevator doors opened, and my words were shelved. I was so dizzy, groggy … Then it was a CT scan, and off I went, rolling from my stretcher onto a slow-moving table.

"Please be still, Mr. Anbar."

Inside that tunnel-like machine, my eyes—and my jumbled brain—succumbed to darkness.

2

Write On

I'm lying on a bed here on the second floor, hooked up to an IV tube and a heart monitor that beeps too frequently. The doors stay open on the Intensive Care Unit, nurses shuffling along the corridors to check on patients. I wish I could get some rest; every few hours they wake me up for another blood test. Last night was a nightmare: when the clock struck midnight, a young RN intern drew blood from me and then carelessly pulled the syringe out of my right arm, spurting all over the sheets. Uggh! Poor girl ... poor me!

I haven't spoken much so far. Last week my wife brought Dr. Seuss' The Cat in the Hat. She sat down on the bed and coaxed me to read out loud. And I did, slowly.

"'I ... have ... no f—fear, says ... th—the ...cat.'"

"'I ... will n—not ... let ... you ff—fall.'"

"'I ... will ... hold ... you ... up ... high.'
"'As ... I ss—stand ... on ... a ... ball.'"

Fuckin' hell! Every word, every broken utterance is like pulling out teeth; every hour that passes, frustration builds close to a boiling point. But I'm making some awesome improvements, day by day. Lots of speech therapy too. Soon my speaking issues won't even be noticeable; the biggest challenge I'll have to face will be my lack of comprehension. But it's okay, I figured, with more hard work maybe I'll get my old self back. Right? I mean, otherwise, what's the point of life? ...

"Good morning, Mr. Anbar. My name is Doctor McKernan. I see you're eating breakfast, that's a good thing!"

"Oh, bon ... giorno, Doc." I moved the tray to the foot of my bed, straightening up. "Very nu—nutritious." I nodded my head, beckoning to a half-eaten turkey sausage and a greasy omelet smeared with a smudge of ketchup. We both chuckled.

"Listen, Mr. Anbar ..."

"Shai," I interrupted. "P ... please."

"Shai. So, Shai, I know it's been now ..." He looked at his med chart. "Three days since your stroke." He put the chart down and sat next to me. "How are you feeling?"

"Been ... worse."

"Okay good, good ... Look, you've been diagnosed with aphasia. You know what aphasia is, don't you?"

"Yeah."

"Well, your aphasia is, luckily, minor. Speech and comprehension are impaired, but you have no serious physical problems. We have to run some more tests, and we're going to monitor your medication and blood samples. Once the underlying cause is addressed, the main treatment for aphasia is speech therapy. So continue with that, keep well, and stay positive. Okay?"

"Okay," I said, and off he went.

Stay positive, huh ... shiiit. I had no way of knowing how many of his words I'd missed. At a guess I'd have said half, or maybe even three-quarters. It was all too damn fast for me to comprehend; it was like turning on the food channel while a radio blared rock, the phone rang, and a doctor talked clinical jive, all at the same time.

I got up from my bed and slowly walked towards the bathroom, my wheeled IV drip stand in tow. I brushed my teeth, took a swig from a mouthwash bottle, gurgled and spat. After washing my face, I grabbed a hospital-issued white bath towel with a blue stripe. A sweet song came to mind, so I sang along softly as I headed back.

"'Well, I ain't al—always right, but I've never … been wrong …'"

Damn it, I couldn't finish the verse. Utterance in incomplete sentences was a bitch and a half. I was about to sit down on my bed, but a sudden sound right behind me made me jump. I turned around.

"What … Who … What are … you doing in my … room?" I cried, baffled. "And why are you … in my ch—chair?"

3

What Planet Did You Come From?

"Sweet lord Zeus, you were singing! Far out, man, I love that tune!" Her voice was bright, mezzo-soprano, but there was something else there, an echo that I couldn't explain. An old memory suddenly hit me: a museum oil painting of Hera, queen of the Olympian gods, sitting upright on an heirloom sofa with red velvet upholstery. Was it at The Met or *Le Louvre*? Her legs were folded sideways, one elbow slightly bent and the other supported on an armrest. She donned a regal, rust-colored dress, its low bust revealing her milky-white complexion. Her head was furtively tilted, eyes large and wise, parted lips framing a pouty mouth.

It surely looked like her. Unless my eyes betrayed me.

"I'm so sorry, I didn't mean to startle you. My name is Aphasia."

I retrieved my glasses from the night table and sat, staring directly at her. "Ex … cuse me?"

"Aphasia," she said calmly, in a matter-of-fact chime. "A-P-H-A-S-I-A. Pronounced 'uh-fay-zha.'"

I must have been hallucinating. "Okay," I said, slowly. "You … you're mm—messing with me, right?"

"Oh, not at all! It's actually a Greek word, it means 'speechless.' Cool name, wouldn't you say?" She grinned.

"So … sorry, you .. lost me," I said, confused. "I have aph—aphasia …"

"That's right!" she exclaimed. "Gosh", she chuckled to herself, "it reminds me of 'Who's on First, What's on Second, I Don't Know is on third.."

My patience was wearing thin. "Look, miss …?"

She shrugged her shoulders innocently. "No last name that I know of."

"Well … then, Aph-asia … No-Last-Name; I'm … Shai Had-E … Nuff." My hard stare intensified. "One time … I mean, one more … time: why the … hell are you … here? And who are you … anyway?"

"Well, it's kind of a long story," she said calmly, "but let's just say that the gods sent me to heal, to love … Wait, I think it must have been Zeus … Jeez, I'm still suffering from some cosmic jet lag.

Anyway, I'll be honest with you," she said, wiping a smile off her face. "I am the thief of words, a scorpion that frogs fall for every time. I don't worry whether people embrace what I am—defects and all—or not, but what I know damn sure is that you, 'aphasians' as you called it, and I—we're in it for the long haul. Nothing prepared you for me barging into your life, and I'm sorry for the precious gifts that you've lost. I'm here to make amends, and my mission now is—"

"Okay stop, stop," I interrupted. "Look ... I don't ... have time for—"

"Let me finish, please," she shot back. "My mission is to show you ... well, as that song goes, 'Get shown the light in the strangest of places ...'"

"'... If you look ... at it ... right,'" I cut her off. Yeah, I know that song—"Scarlet Begonia" by The Grateful Dead. "Wh ... what are you supp—supposed to show me ... exactly?"

"I'm going to show you how beautiful you are, inside and out. I'll show you what you already know, but never paid attention to till I came into your life. When we go down together into the deep, dark cave of your mind, I will bring a lamp and light it for you."

"Can we ... stop this ch—charade, please?" I said. "It was nice ... nice talking to you ... really. I ... wish you ... the vv—very best." I gestured to the door. "Now would ... you mind ...?"

"You're so grumpy!" Aphasia sulked. "Look, I'm .. I don't know how to say it ..."

"For ff—fuck's sake!"

"Okay, okay." She put her hands up. "I'm your companion."

"My ... what?" I said, incredulously. "Wh—what does that mean? That we're—"

"You know," she cut me off, "in conjunction, side by side, hand in hand, simultaneous, in concert, not separate ..."

"Holy ... crap, am I ... stuck? With ... you?" I said, still digesting.

"Well, I wouldn't necessarily say that ..."

"Am I!?" I cried out.

"Yes, Shai." Aphasia turned serious. "I'm afraid so."

My brain slammed on the brakes, wheels screeching, manual shift grinding to a parked halt.

"Hello?" she said, cautiously. A few more seconds went by. "Shai?"

Tick. Tock. Tick. Tock.

"Please say something ..."

"Are you ... for real?" I asked, coldly.

"Whew, thank the gods. You scared me."

"ARE YOU!?"

"Hmmm ... Well, that depends."

"Depends on ... goddamn what?" I blurted out.

"Depends on you. Your disability is real, yet the doors and windows of your mind and your disposition are for you to close or open. You can bring in things like imagination and inspiration. Or you can kick those two out, if you insist."

Unfucking believable. I mean, look who the cat dragged in! Here I am with a dented brain talking to myself in gibberish and who comes to my rescue? The Goddess of Language Disorder!

"I'm not a goddess, not yet anyway. I'm still earning my laurels," Aphasia continued, twinkling in jest. "Call me 'a goddess in training' for now."

"What the hell ... are you?" I solemnly said.

"I don't know," she said, shrugging. "Am I a scorpion? Maybe a chameleon? Nah, unlike me, they are solitary animals." She then got serious. "In some ways, I'm a double-edged sword. Definitely a condition, a cruel, devastating one. I'm not driven by malice or ingratitude, but rather by an unconquerable and indiscriminate need to hurt. But I'm also a partner, a humble servant, and a silent, self-possessed mistress. And yes, a real pain in the ass—way too often. I admit it—I'm a high-maintenance random friend and I wouldn't be surprised if you decide to characterize me as a cunning foe. But you mean the world to me. I wish I could be a good goddess to you."

"Perish the ... thought," I mumbled.

Aphasia smiled. "C'mon. cheer up. Tell you what—here's a secret I'll share with you. Ready?"

I was exhausted. "Can't ... fuckin' wait," I said, sarcastically.

"I have a sister. Her name is Elpis. I wish you two could have met, but that won't be possible. Busy bee she is, always pollinating!" Aphasia chuckled, then went on. "Our mom, Nyx—'the goddess of night', the one who stood at the beginning of creation, mind you—gave birth to many deities like me and my sister. Bright, young, usually carrying flowers or a cornucopia in her hands—Elpis is a one-of-a-kind because she's always able to see that there's light despite all the darkness. There are cracks in everything, and light can always get in. Me, I'm the pragmatist; she's the ultimate optimist. She has a burning passion for the possible."

And I thought *you*, Aphasia, were supposed to show me the light, I muttered to myself. Elpis, huh ... sounds like a brand-name prescription drug that's used for treating venereal disease.

Aphasia laughed wildly, then calmed down. "Her name in Greek mythology means 'the spirit of Hope,'" she said.

Silly me, I get it. A bolt of lightning flashed in my brain, then seamlessly translated into a thought. For just one fleeting moment, I could imagine myself: Aphasia and a spirit of hope, *un ménage à trois par excellence.* But I've always been a skeptic. It's as if there's a devil on my right shoulder nudging me, saying, *"Hey pal, you've never been an advocate for hope and you've always preferred a 'do it yourself' approach, so don't wait for hope to save your ass!"* Then there's an angel on my left, assuring me that unlike words, hope is the last thing ever lost: "*If you have hope on your side, you can become an agent of change, growth and renewal. Go, confront things and commit to evolving. Remember, as far as hope goes, there's always a silver lining.*"

Oh boy ... Aphasia and Hope: the glass half-empty and the glass half-full. Hope can wish things all it wants and my aphasia is definitely not going away; it is I who have to make the impossible possible. The question is, am I ready for some honest coexistence between the two?

"All I know, Aph-phasia ... for sure is ... I'm definitely fucked. Ex—excuse my French," I growled.

"Sans souci, mon ami!" Aphasia tweeted. "You don't need to Apollo-gize!" she winked. "Relax your brow, Sir Croakes-a-lot. Yeah, we're companions, whether we like it or not, but let's let our hair down and explore. Let's see what the roads of life offer us!"

"No ... too many ... roads are closed now—"

"—and others can be opened!" said Aphasia, adamant. "You know what 'neuroplasticity' is? Let me do the honors. It's the ability of neural networks in your brain to change through growth and reorganization. Your brain is like a ball of clay that you can mold and shape. So many characteristics can be modified and adjusted, but it requires work!"

"Ww—work, you say?" I went on with my

taunting. "Too bad. Thanks to ... you, I'll be joi—joining the ... ranks of the ... unemployed."

Aphasia rolled her eyes, inhaled and exhaled. "Can you shelve your sarcasm just for a second, for once in your life? Look, I don't want to get too medical, but with a remodeled brain, you have the capacity to retain memories, improve motor function, enhance comprehension and speech. And yes, it does take work: learning, practicing, and stimulating through activities. Therapy, for example. I'm tipping my hat to you for trying," Aphasia said. "Just keep on keepin' on! Your neurological pathways are not closed; just think outside of the box. We do have our companionship. Which reminds me of a poem I love. Guess who wrote this one:

I'm Nobody! Who are you?
Are you – Nobody – too?
Then there's a pair of us!
Don't tell! they'd advertise – you know!
How dreary – to be – Somebody!
How public – like a Frog –"

"Yeah, yeah, I ... know." I cut her off. "Emily ... Dickinson." Speaking of frogs, I guess her and Aphasia are making sure I'll never become a prince no matter how many kisses I get. "Look," I said, "I'm ... tired. Can you just ... leave me ... alone, please?"

"Sure thing. Ribbit." She chuckled. "On one condition."

"Which is ... ?"

"I want you to write," Aphasia implored. "You can always converse with me—you know, inner speech and all— but when you don't feel like talking, or can't, then just keep writing. I'll sit back quietly and enjoy it. I'm a very good listener, you know." She smiled.

My insecurity crept up instantly. I wasn't sure what the point of writing was. I couldn't even tell you how frustrating that process sounds. Especially now.

"Can I be a little selfish?" said Aphasia, unfolding her legs and leaning closer. "The reason I beg you to write is because it's you who can bring out more awareness and exposure about me. About the people who are living with and caring for those with your condition." She winked. "I want you to make me famous, you know what I'm sayin'?"

"Sure," I scoffed. "I can't wait to ... see your ff—fugly face on my ... Wheaties box."

She gave me a ringing staccato laugh. "Here's a question for you, wise guy: how many people know about me?"

"A ... few?"

"Too few!

" ... and you want me to ... make you f—famous by ... writing my sto—story?"

"Yours, yes, and mine. Better yet, ours."

I paused for a brief moment, then derision sprang to the surface. I could see the headlines: "Survivors Shai and Aphasia are storming your town! Just beware, folks: *the heart and the head are, by nature, enemies!*" Do I seriously expect me to put my chagrin aside and promote ... her?

"Why not?" she said. "Just add some water, a little self-awareness, and stir."

"I detect ... a tinge of ... conceit?"

"For good reason!" she charged, before softening her tone. "I'm like a genie in a bottle. If you can uncork it and release me, then look out, world! Just as long as you tell your tales."

Must be the bottle with a skull and crossbones label, right? I sneered. "What if ... I don't?"

"Then why write at all, if sharing is not in your vocabulary?"

I squinted. "What ... tales you want me to ... tell?"

"Anything and everything. Write what makes you feel good, and if writing helps take the load off your troubled mind, then by all means do so. You want to vent some? Vent on! Vent on me, that's what I'm here for! Do you want to laugh at me or with me? Wanna cry? Whine? All of the above? Go for it, man, unleash your pains! I'm hearing you, listening to you, helping you to value yourself, to feel empowered and inspired.

It's all in you. You have all the time in the world,

so you can do it at your own pace." She winked at me and chirped, "You get my drift?"

There was something about her—or it?—that was starting to put me at ease. Sure, her traumatic emergence into my life hadn't sunk in yet, but in a bizarre way, for a fleeting moment, my mind conceded that maybe, just maybe, Aphasia could be a ..

Companion? Nope, I was still in denial.

Friend? No fuckin' way. If I want one, I'll get a dog.

How about the co-writer of my life story?

My train of thought had reached the station. I came back to reality. Okay, I will write. Write because I can, because my pen can be my saber, letting my inspiration flow. Write because I should; the more I open up, the more I tell the whole world about Aphasia so that everyone can benefit. That she-devil can hold a mirror up to me, reminding me of what I already know but too often forget. She's my darkest shadow, my mental state in a flux, the yin to her yang. All those dimensions can be viewed through the lens of my condition, as long as I'm willing to tell our story, to spread *the Word*.

So I'm writing away, and no, I won't ever give up. Aphasia is my curse, but—even a little—she's partly my blessing. If I give it a chance, maybe she'll show me the light.

Right now, I really want my melancholy back and to sulk for a bit. "Can you go ... back to ...

your home pp—planet, Aphasia, and ... leave me alone?"

"Wish I could," she said, leaning back on my chair. "But it's your time to give voice, so I promise—from now on, mum's the word. Just remember, my arms are always open for you, troubadour, no matter what!"

4

In Purgatory

Winter, 2012.

Outside it's pouring, merciful tears washing away the burden of the day. Notes from a trumpet next door pierce through a curtain of wetness, dissonant and coarse. When I moved into a small, sparsely-furnished attic right next to Presby Iris Garden, so did my neighbor, who is an aspiring trumpet player. From a broken sequence of scales to an uphill struggle with John Coltrane, my ears have faithfully—if unwillingly—borne witness.

I was pacing aimlessly back and forth. Dusk, painted in hues of blue, had reluctantly yielded to another cold, wet and dark night. I could feel my demons and their clowns putting on their makeup, getting ready for some painful circus show that I would have to endure. Visions of pure personal hell flashed before my eyes, ripping my splintering mind apart.

It was exactly one year after my stroke, but the fog hadn't dissipated and my comprehension had given way to utter despondency. My brain's circuitry was cut short, as if someone had unplugged all the wires in my fuse box—sparking fire, the smell of smoke. My constant torment haunted me, a deep ache filled with emotions that I couldn't express. I would have done anything for some sense of clarity, coherence, or quietness. But I couldn't, I simply couldn't. I wished distractions would go away; I wished I could think straight instead of zigzagging, changing lanes recklessly in the middle of my neurological highway. The potholes in my broken syntax were unfixable. The yellow sign on my street of dreams read "Under Construction," but the Union was on strike. I could barely understand anything anymore.

Christ, I didn't know *me*. I didn't recognize myself, I didn't know who or what I was. I'd been a contributor, a working man, a family man. Now look what I'd become: freshly separated from my wife, a homeless-for-the-heart scavenger living off crumbs of success and happiness. I tried not to indulge in self-pity; I certainly couldn't blame anyone or anything for my stroke. But my deafening cry reverberated within my walls, echoing, "Why me!?" Or, better yet, "Why?" The man I used to be vanished under sedation, everything unraveling before my eyes. No happiness, no contentment, no peace, no job, no friends, no wife, no point. My grief, my loss and bereavement over the "old me," my identity and my self-esteem, all were shot to pieces. My healthy inner self? Give me a break; it was all a colossal losing proposition.

Six steps from my futon, I took a U-turn to my cheap Ikea desk, stopping at my fridge to pop open a cold Blue Ribbon beer. Another brisk left turn, three steps to my single chair, lighting another Marlboro, then three more steps to a window that had an obstructed view to a busy street. Then back to square one. There wasn't a kitchen in my apartment because my town's fire marshal said so. No TV because I didn't need one; why waste time watching movies or series when I'd lose half of any story's gist? No pictures mounted on the walls because the attic was triangular, and the only one I'd plastered on the ceiling was an unframed poster of Paco de Lucia, a famous Spanish flamenco guitarist. His eyes were closed, face pained and sorrowful, fingers stamped on the ebony neck of his guitar.

I felt trapped like a prisoner on death row, waiting for the hangman's mercy but instead sentenced to a torturous stay of execution. Somehow, I turned off the volume inside my head, replacing static white noise with a blank, empty screen. No words were spoken. My wheel stopped spinning, as if a silent black-and-white movie reel, totally out of focus, had been cut short. No shadows haunted me, no visuals whatsoever. Mental exhaustion and valium had done the trick; I was fading fast.

There was no solace or pity in the night for me. Heavens' tears were unfazed, unimpressed, transcendental. It has already silenced the sound of a trumpet and was ready to substitute darkness with light. Chopin played softly on my radio; dawn's subtle fingers seduced the key of E Minor into a requiem. At the bottom of a near-empty beer can, my last cigarette hissed and died. I crumpled onto my futon, exhausted. Shut-eye was my catharsis, nothingness was my bliss.

5

Routine

Me? Depressed? C'mon, Doc! Why are you shaking your head? I know, my ideal weight for years was around 184 pounds. Today's reading? Twenty pounds less. But hey, who's complaining, right? I mean, it's not like my condition—you know, my stroke that happened last year—hasn't impacted my appetite. When my marriage was on the brink and I moved out from our family home, the smells that had emanated from my kitchen suddenly dissipated. My vast arsenal of cooking tools took a sabbatical, sitting dormant in an attic closet. The laughter at dinner, mingled with jingling silverware, turned to an unbearable silence. No wonder I haven't eaten much.

Don't get me wrong, Doc, cooking was my religion, a close second only to soccer, but it was always about sharing. Who could I share with when my aphasia came in and solitude hit? I tell you, for us Anbar men—my dad, his brother, my younger brother, even my son—our kitchens have always been our kingdoms. The minute we got home after work, business suits or construction gear shifted to aprons and towels slung over our shoulders. If music and poetry were my private sanctuary, cooking was my family's. Imagination, innovation, but more importantly, love and giving—that was our highest authority.

Pardon me, Doc? Oh, you're asking about my Aphasia? She's my new companion, an odd bird alright. When she twisted my arm to go out for lunch, that was the straw that broke the camel's back.

It was the first time after my stroke that we'd ventured out to the local diner, leaving my frozen meals and junk food out. Our waitress was young, pretty, and dressed in a black uniform. She grinned and said, "Hi there, Sir. How are you today? My name is Violet. Our specials today are Hampshire pogajsg jshbdj with ghdbbs sauce, grilled djfdh gillet and Angus stridgd New York katsjj. Would you like an appetizer first?"

"Run that by ... me again, Va—Violet? I said. I actually had to sneak a peek at another customer's plate across my booth. "Nah, just ... kiddin'. A Greek ss—salad will do." But man, what an embarrassment! I should have studied the menu, which isn't exactly easy for me to do, and pointed at a particular dish. Violet could have given me the silent sign of approval. No wonder we didn't go back.

In truth, my speech and my comprehension are a bit better now. I make some intelligible sense and I get the gist of things if someone doesn't talk too fast or for too long. But as my aphasia can testify, mixing those two ingredients—talking and understanding? That's the toxic combination that causes me to lose my appetite.

But all is not lost, Doc. I've got news for you: I'm moving to a slightly bigger apartment because—drum roll, please—it has a tiny kitchen! One thing I can say for sure is that my condition has taken me to another level when it comes to the culinary arts. After all, I have tons of free time on my hands, being unemployed and all. So, I figured, why not use that time to get deeper into cooking, with more vigor, creativity and resourcefulness? Mind you, I'm a passionate, obsessive chef, and I wear many different hats: Middle Eastern, European, you name it. Take my Yemenite beef bone soup, for example—enjoy the loud sucking noises when you vacuum up that exquisite marrow. Why not try my stellar shepherd's pie? Creamy mashed potatoes, a heavenly fusion of ground lamb and beef, and enough spices to make you do a jig. Or my lasagna, a triple-decker veggie with my secret red sauce. *Madonna Santa,* if the angels in heaven don't serve lasagna at least as good as mine, then I ain't going! Feeling like snacking instead, Doc? *No hay problema*; you wanna open a bag of tortilla chips and crack a bottle of Dos Equis? My secret jalapeno sauce—whether mild or hot, your call—*Carajo, delicioso!* Let's spice up life, shall we?

You're asking me if I speak Spanish, Doc? ¡*Sí señor!* Linguistics has always been one of my true passions. My mother tongue was Hebrew, but as a child I had a huge appetite for curiosity and wanted to learn English. In the 60s, we didn't learn a secondary language in school until we were in the fourth grade. Luckily for me, this was about the same time Beatlemania took the world by storm. When I bought their albums and listened to their tunes, I meticulously dissected their lyrics. Armed with my bible—a hardcover English-Hebrew dictionary—I wanted to understand The Beatles' song, *Across the Universe*, and its lyrics—*'Pools of sorrow, waves of joy are drifting through my open mind, Possessing and caressing me.'* Every time I lay down in bed and stared at John Lennon's poster hanging on my wall, I thought, "I learned something new. I want to learn more." In a short time I became bilingual.

But I was never finished with languages—far from it. When I enrolled in high school in the States, I had to choose another language to learn. I picked German. Three years, straight As. In college, my new elective was Russian. Da, Comrade! Four years, the usual As. Shifting gears from academics to the business world, I lived in Belgium and studied French and Flemish. I then spent a few years living in Tuscany. I was so proficient in honing my Italian that this language became second nature.

Here comes Spanish, Doc. When I moved to Miami, I became totally immersed in the culture—the fascinating Latin American vibe. I believed that only through language could I feel like I truly belonged. Perfecting my Spanish would mean little if I didn't know or care about important issues like immigration, equality and violence, to name a few. I wanted to be part of a community that not only spoke the same language, but also tried to close racial gaps through understanding, respect and harmony. Oh and, of course, food.

I was on a mission. I immediately bought a dictionary, a grammar book, a Berlitz book and some Rosetta Stone tapes. I also bought a book called *Chistes Pelados*—dirty jokes. I religiously attended festivities in Little Havana, like the carnival, and always made time to enjoy salsa music and rueda dancing. I hung out in South Beach very frequently, drinking margaritas while I watched some curvy, jaw-dropping *nenas calientes*. One thing's for sure: I didn't want to be some fuckin' tourist, a gringo wearing plaid shorts and tube socks with a camera hanging around his neck. I wanted to look the part: a guayabera shirt and panama hat, a Montecristo cigar fixed between my lips, and an *El Nuevo Herald* tucked under my arm. I wanted to burst that damn window wide open, mastering the language and expanding my cultural horizons.

That's all over now. I can't speak Italian and or Spanish anymore. I'm not giving up—I read *La Gazzetta dello Sport* and *El País* newspapers online, and I practice my vocabulary daily. My Hebrew and English survived—slightly fractured, a little nervous from the fall. I joined yet another speech group, but my heart was broken. I lost my beloved languages, and I found aphasia instead.

So no, Doc, I ain't starving. I know I'm not the picture of health, but I keep a pretty healthy appetite—nothing deep-fried, no sugar, easy on the gluten. I do fall off the wagon now and then. I sometimes need a break from nonstop chit-chat with my brain; when the sun goes down and it's Miller Time, I flee from my nest. Three minutes later a Yuengling pint, a *Cuervo* tequila shot—no salt, yes lime—and the old familiar murmur and bustle of Tierney's tavern put us totally at ease. Then comes the cherry on top: their majestic chili fries with cheese, the best in all New Jersey. Damn sinful! Perfect fries, just the right cut; sweet and tangy chili crafted by Buddy the Chef; a good dose of melted cheddar cheese that bonds our souls ...

Lordy Lord, I'm a-cumin'! No wonder I go and light up a cigarette after a foodgasm like that.

But okay, Doc, you've won the battle hands down—I promise I'll behave. I'll gain some weight, eat healthier, maybe cut down on the antidepressants and anti-anxiety prescriptions and stop smoking. Everything is aphasia's damn fault, ain't it, but I'll make the effort. Know what I'm sayin', Doc? *Yo me voy, hombre*; I'll bid you goodbye and go on my miserable, merry way.

6

Flunked Out

Am I sorry for having left culinary school?
Well, besides getting a refund on my tuition at a prestigious institution, going home with my tail between my legs and hating myself a little bit more, all is good..

I enrolled … What, a year or so after my stroke? Cooking in a classroom for hours, standing on my feet, my classmates, all of them half my age ….Wait. Half my age? More like two-thirds, the old geezer I was. Most of them looked like they were under the legal drinking age. I kid, but in truth, camaraderie was absent. It would have been nice to have colleagues who could lend me a hand. Not even physically but mentally, because the most important factor my comprehension lacked was attention to detail. Grasping a barrage of culinary information, materials, facts and figures, not to mention cramming texts for upcoming exams ... It was almost like learning a new language.

The curriculum was vast: knife skills, palate development and herb identification, mixing up stocks, soups, sauces, reductions and emulsifications ... Exploring dry and moist heat methods like braising, grilling, and roasting, getting experience with ingredients, techniques and dishes from all over the world, experimenting with cured meats and so much more. We had instructors from well-known restaurants, culinary technology labs outfitted with old-fashioned and modernist equipment, management training for restaurant operators and aspiring entrepreneurs, hands-on externships and networking opportunities, job placement services and ongoing alumni support. All we had to do was roll up our sleeves and immerse ourselves.

The moment we arrived at that school building, each of us had to fend for ourselves. We'd change clothes in the locker rooms, and we always dressed for battle: a puffy junior chef's cap, checkered pants, a white apron and buttoned-up coat, a pair of black non-slip leather clogs and two school-issued blue side towels. The only thing we weren't allowed to wear was a smile. The instructor, Robert, might as well have been a sergeant major impersonating a chef, and his soldiers—my classmates—were scared shitless. If you added too much salt you would have to give him twenty push-ups.

"'Get to your workstation!'" he barked. "'Now listen up! Béchamel sauce, I just wrote it down on the blackboard! 2 tablespoons butter, 2 tablespoons flour, 1¼ cup heated milk. You have one minute. Go!'"

The poor youngsters headed for the cupboards and closets, scampering frantically, scavenging for precious ingredients while almost coming to blows. But I was still frozen, trying to memorize how much butter I needed or what the quarter was. Everybody hurried back to their stations, and he looked at me and then addressed the minions. "You see? When it comes to cooking, time is of the essence. Preparation, punctuality, that's what counts! And here's a good example of how important it is!" Then he pointed at me ...

The bastard. I should have hit him on the head with a cast-iron skillet. But I'm a graduate of anger management, with honors, mind you; I'm still proud that I made an effort—a huge one. My mistake was being too embarrassed to tell Robert about my aphasia. A couple of months into the course, during a twenty-minute smoke break, he and I were sitting down on the fire escape. For just a minute we were alone, and I was so close to telling him ... but I couldn't. I flicked my cigarette butt and went back inside. Two days later I quit.

I wonder though, What would I do differently now?

For starters, how about if I stop feeling sorry for myself and never stop cooking? Dealing with this new reality—my disability and all—is a bitch and a half, but so can I. Don't stop the world just because you want to get off. Metaphorically speaking, of course.

Food for thought, damn it.

PART II

My Private War

7

Pet Peeve

I need to vent, aphasians. Buckle up.

I saw a sticker recently that said, "Aphasia: Loss of Words, Not Intellect." It kind of vexes my ass, and I'll tell you why. First, we know that aphasia is mainly a speech disability. Making sense out of words becomes like pulling teeth; the construction of each argument comes out totally upside down, or sideways, or backwards. It's a moot point of discussion, right, but why bring intellect up at all? Unless, as I suspect, it's about the large chip on our shoulders; we're embarrassed to see people pitying us. To be blunt, we can tell what they're thinking: 'They're all over the place, they hardly speak; I wonder, are they disabled?' I get it, but to react with a sticker like that .. give me a break! We might as well shout, *We're fucked, but we're still smart!*

And that's where the second part comes in: since we've decided to advertise our intellect, are we really as smart as we used to be? I know the lab rat neurologists and speech therapists would genuinely say so. But if we truly stand on even ground and are not intellectually inferior to the rest of the world, then why do we stop mattering to them? Why do we become irrelevant?

Here's an example for you, a true story. A few months after my stroke, when I was technically a CEO—I wasn't fired yet but I was put on leave—I put a suit on, grabbed my leather briefcase, and drove up to Boston to meet my executive team. My agenda was to reunite with all of my employees and get filled in on the sales projections for our monthly budget. After smiles and handshakes galore, it was finally time to sit down in the conference room and get back to business. My staff took turns updating me about the numbers, the customers, the travel engagements and so on.

An hour later, we were done. I didn't ask them any questions. I didn't disagree with any input they gave. My wise words in the discourse amounted to "Sounds ... good," "Not bad," and my favorite: "Ummm." Oh, and the last and only unstuttered sentence I ended with was, "I'll get back to you." Because me and my aphasia were in la-la land. I understood maybe twenty percent of what it was all about. See, I could hear what they were saying, but I couldn't process it into a coherent business-like discourse.

I was so embarrassed, I just wanted to go home and never come back to work. I take that back; I did entertain the possibility of flipping burgers for a living, but making quick decisions like "with pickles or without?" would have been too much to comprehend. At least they put me out of my misery by firing me. Maybe I should have worn a button that read "I'm useless; please shoot first, ask questions never."

There were tons of other embarrassing episodes that I shouldn't mention. Okay, if you must: I went to Starbucks and tried to order a latte; the people behind me would roll their eyes in despair. Same for the cashiers at my supermarket and the staff at the movie theater. I just wondered, does Aphasia relish in my helplessness?

Maybe I'm making a big deal out of this. But it matters to me. It's not debatable whether aphasians are intellectually impaired. The problem dwells at the boundaries of language and thought. To a certain extent they're inseparable, which makes the loss of language a double whammy when it comes to framing and understanding ideas. And if you can't understand such a simple connection, then why on earth would you keep harping on about intellect? You know what I'm saying? We are fighters, not Einsteins! But here's the beautiful thing that ol'

Albert said: "The intellect has little to do on the road to discovery. There comes a leap in consciousness, call it intuition or what you will, the solution comes to you and you don't know how or why." Blew my fuckin' mind! I'd gladly put up a sign that says, "Aphasia: Loss of Language, Not Intuition."

It reminds me of the Dead song "Terrapin Station." 'Inspiration, move me brightly,' it goes, 'Light the song with sense and color, hold away despair." And what's the next verse? "Statements just seem vain at last." As hard as we may try, the words we use to cloak our insecurities often wind up revealing them. I know I'd much rather wave banners promoting humility instead of self-doubt.

The moral story? Intellect is a lot like underwear: it's important that you have it, but not necessary that you show it off...

8

Charred Memories

It must be Friday, before the Sabbath. I'm sitting on a bus headed for home. Dressed in dusty fatigues, my longing for comfort itches as terribly as my scruffy beard. As the wheels keep on turning, I slouch in my seat, close my eyes and do my damndest, in vain, to think at all.

It was Saturday, June 5, 1982, only six months after I finished my mandatory three years of army service in the IDF (Israeli Defense Forces). That day was unusual. As I laid spread-eagle on the beach—a long, half-mile strip of white sand dunes bordered by rocks, caves, marras grass and hens and chicks plants—working on my tan, helicopters and jet planes thronged over gunboats sailing swiftly on the water. All those war machines were headed north, bound for Lebanon. Many people on the beach had brought portable radios to listen to the news. The message was clear: the operation had officially begun. But the conflict was limited in scale, as far as we knew, with no massive enlistment of reserve soldiers. Reservists like me knew that the probability of getting a call from the army and being ordered to report for duty was slim. In the meantime, why not enjoy a glorious Sabbath and cash in on precious leisure time?

At midnight, my parents bid me goodnight and went upstairs. I was twenty-two at the time, living at home while looking for an apartment of my own. I took a long, relaxing shower and read more of my latest book, but soon felt exhausted. I put the book down, reached for my reading light and closed my eyes.

Ring-ring! Ring-ring! Ring-ring! My dad answered the phone. Thirty seconds later he hung up, turned the lights on and came downstairs. I'd been drafted. I got up, opened my closet, put on my combat uniform and stuffed my kitbag with the essentials: a few pairs of underwear, colorful dancing bears socks, a carton of Noblesse cigarettes and a handful of marzipan chocolate bars. Twenty minutes later, there was a knock on our door. I hugged and kissed my parents, bid them *L'hitraot* and climbed onto an army van.

Eventually we arrived at a military supply base, filing out and sitting along with other reservists on the open ground. We waited.

And waited.

And waited some more.

I looked at my watch—it was 4 a.m. I hadn't slept a wink.

Finally, a high-ranking officer approached us. "ATTEN-TION!" he barked. We all rose from our slumber, straightened our backs and saluted.

"Listen up, truck drivers. You were the last ones needed, but as you can see, we're running low on vehicles. You may have to wait here until something comes up; no telling how long that'll be. For now, one artillery regiment that has already crossed the border desperately needs a truck. All I have is this one." He pointed to a revved-up, prepped-and-ready Mercedes-Benz gasoline tanker pulling out of a bay. "Any volunteers?"

The officer looked around, scanning. Nobody spoke a word.

Fuck it, I'd had enough. "I'll go," I said, raising my hand.

I have no idea why I did it. Maybe it was the thrill of adventure that increased my heart rate. Or it might have been my moral compass; they needed me, after all, and I was already there.

"Come with me," the officer said. I climbed up, adjusted my seat and my mirrors. Next thing I knew, I was shifting gears and heading towards the unknown.

Only a few days later, I was part of a convoy

driving to Baalbek, a city situated in the Beqqa Valley. Once we arrived, I looked around in astonishment. What a magnificent landscape Lebanon was! Green hills and pristine valleys, snow-capped mountains, olive groves and sleepy, picturesque villages dotted with mosques and monasteries. As we drove on, locals waved their arms, showering us with tokens and gestures of goodwill. Wicker baskets full of cherries, bushels of rice, shouts of thanks and praise. I could feel the suspicion and animosity that lurked beneath—hints of fear on their faces, young and old—but I felt at ease. I'd already lived up to my end of the bargain by offering them my respect and participating in this senseless war.

I open my eyes. Man, that forty-day tour of duty is already over! The bus inches its way to the terminal's depot in my hometown, Rishon. The wheels screech, the engine dies. I'm home.

I sling my kitbag over one shoulder, cross my rifle on the other, and hit the ground. It's a beautiful day, not too hot, and I smell the intoxicating fragrance of citrus blossoms from our town's abundance of orchard groves. I smile and start walking, genial and lighthearted, passing my old familiar haunts: a small bakery full of breads and pastries; Deborah's Kiosk, even smaller, that boasts her homemade popsicles; a patch of dirt next to our childhood home that we used as a makeshift soccer field.

At long last I reach my destination, our small steel gate with fenced-in, semi-manicured bushes. I unbolt the latch with a screech, walk in and bolt it again, then start on the short cobblestone path towards the front door. To my left is a white jasmine tree where Pluto, our family dog, was buried. Right by the door is the skinny, two-story mandarin tree that bears fruit in bushels. It's strange there aren't any "Welcome Home" banners outside, but it doesn't matter; I'm so excited. I open the door and walk in.

The place is bare. All those pictures that my dad had painted and mounted on our walls are gone. There's no furniture whatsoever, no framed family photos. The Persian rug is no longer on the checkerboard floor of our living room.

Mom isn't here. Neither is dad. It's so cold I'm shivering. Total silence engulfs me.

Suddenly there's a deafening explosion. I cringe, closing my eyes, my hands instinctively covering my ears. When I rise up and open my eyes, I'm no longer at our family home; instead, I'm back in Lebanon, back in the war. The firing continues and thousands of bombs make for an absolutely devastating refrain. The measured cadence of the constant bombardment begins to drill into the corners of my brain.

It feels like an eternity until it finally stops. A sinister quiet and the thick smell of gunpowder descend upon me. I look in terror at the once majestic land now turned into a smoky battlefield. I survey the scorched earth before me; the carnage is atrocious. There are corpses everywhere: some inside bunkers, others in foxholes, some more belly-up or face-down on the ground. Legs, arms, and small pieces of flesh are scattered over ashen rocks and caught in tree branches. Some bodies are charred and disfigured, others torn to shreds. Buzzards fill the air.

I feel sick to my stomach. I want to be numb, but ... I just can't.

Wait. Who is that figure, the one laying down, half hidden by a rock?

I slowly take one step, stop, then take another. My heartbeat sounds like a galloping horse. I'm getting closer.

And closer.

Oh my god, he's moving. Is this ... Dad? Is this ...

I woke up, gasping for air. My heartbeat was racing, cold sweating rolling from my brow. I glanced at my alarm clock—it was 6 a.m. I looked out from my window. The sky was layered with purple, blue, and orange. My brain stopped screeching, giving way to an unusual serenity.

I slowly sat up. I'm groggy. I need coffee.

Do I wanna talk about it? Sure. But please, coffee first.

9

The Trauma Club

Sometimes we aphasians don't have many ways out. There are traumatic events outside of our control—strokes, the death of loved ones—but we are survivors, true warriors who choose to fight the good fight, to treat our battles as winnable. We mourn losses—of language, of friends, of human lives—but they make us stronger. And when we find ourselves in deep distress, we have the courage and the will to open our floodgates, letting sadness out and compassion in.

Just like my stroke, my experience in the Lebanon War was a more private affair—perhaps too much so. Us soldiers—just like us aphasians—need to know how warfare feels and how to express, confront, and cross our turbulent rivers. If we do, then we can teach others, finding contentment and a genuine sense of purpose.

I used to think adventure found me, rather than the other way round. I was ten or eleven years old when a tour guide took us hiking in the Golan Heights—a hilly region overlooking the Jordan River that Israel occupied in 1967 having won the Six-Day War—for our class trip. Our teacher, Margo, warned us to fall in line and never leave her side. As we trekked towards a beautiful waterfall, I beckoned two buddies of mine to follow and we veered off onto a shortcut. A few minutes later, as we walked downhill, Margo and the tour guide spotted us. They waved their hands frantically, pointing towards the path that the three of us had ignored. Unbeknownst to us, we were skirting a minefield—totally unmarked. Fortunately we made it safely to the base of the waterfall, where we rejoined the group. Poor Margo berated us in public but I've never forgotten that sense of bravery, that buzz of the risk, the feeling of total freedom.

How, then, did I have the courage to face the fear of uncertainty? Part of it must have been my personal "black box": the electrical, chemical, and neural network of inputs and outputs that wired my genetic structure. But hey, we're not machines. It's up to us to dig deeper and understand ourselves better. I'm not a gambler or a restless seeker of danger; what's in my nature is exploration. I always wanted to know more, learn more, experiment more. I wasn't the kind to anxiously wait for the next adventure. If mystery or uncertainty piqued my interest—in love, in war—I tended to grab hold with both hands.

Traumas are not our fault, aphasians, but it is our responsibility to embrace who and what we are. Let's seize our moment. Oh, how rich, how awe-inspiring our internal landscape is!

———

Some minefields typically last longer than the conflicts they are used in, becoming remnants of war. I was never able to completely vanquish the haunting images of the battlefield, those visions of hell that scarred my memory. I do have my scars, though dealing with my aphasia just might be on the same level. But it's alright. I guess if I survived war, I can survive anything. Having trouble sleeping, feeling worthless with tons of fatalism, the dependence on pharmaceuticals—sounds familiar, doesn't it? But there was one good thing I did that changed my life before I had my stroke. You'd think I would have been happier to leave the war behind, but new demons—anxiety and boredom—moved in immediately. I mean, there I was at twenty-two, still living with my parents, with no real plans for a future. Until …

Refill the popcorn bucket, pop another soda. It's showtime!

10

My Winter of Discontent

On an unseasonably cold night in January 1983, my childhood friend Nir, my teammate "Stretch"—a 6-foot 9-inch basketball player—and I were "sitting" at Nir's house. By sitting I mean getting high, of course. We took turns passing the bong around, laughing our butts off until our stomachs hurt and our eyes streamed with hysterical tears. Hours later, Stretch and I bid *adieu* to our gracious host and staggered off, still raging against the dying of the light.

After that, Stretch and I went to work cleaning apartment buildings in town. He usually picked me up at my house in the early morning hours. Coffees-to-go and a shared joint was our customary wake-up call, a damn good start to the day. Out came the buckets, sponges, brooms, and mops, not to mention our rolling laughter echoing down the halls.

Nighttime meant "sitting" again at Nir's, Stretch's, or whoever. Rinse and repeat.

My treat was going out alone to Tel Aviv, usually landing at a nightclub called The Penguin for some good avant-garde live music. We'd gone together at first, but my buddies had since tied knots with their remarkably loving other halves. I, always the singleton, had little choice but to put on some eyeliner and head out. I'd hop in my old, cranky lime-green Renault 4 that my dad bought me when I came back from the war as a present, turn the ignition on and insert a cassette tape. Bauhaus' "Bela Lugosi's Dead" would blare loudly while I rolled a joint with one hand—a craft I'd perfected—and took the wheel with the other. I'd light, inhale, exhale, relax and coast. Yup, another typical sleepless night for an unwise owl like me.

But there was something missing in my idle, seemingly idyllic life that nagged at me to no end. Playing ball, soaking up sun and sea, getting high, getting laid—those were all fine and dandy, but they made me wonder: was that *it*? What had happened to the popular, confident mama's boy destined for greatness? Let's look at his brief curriculum vitae, starting in Israel: ranked among the top of his class in elementary school; placed first in the city's geography contest; and played the accordion, guitar and drums. Then, as a teenager in the U.S.: lived and breathed basketball, won multiple trophies, graduated high school early, made the Dean's List, lost his virginity, enrolled in college at seventeen, and picked up a leading role in Rutgers' dramatic play, called—of all things—"Bury the Dead" by Irwin Shaw.

That glorified resume told just part of the story. In 1975, my dad got a three-year assignment working for the Jewish Agency, so our family moved to Cherry Hill, New Jersey. My formative years—ages fifteen to eighteen—shaped me in many ways. I was in love with America. When we packed our bags heading for home, I decided that after my military service, I'd return, finish college, and make a happier, better life for myself.

Fast forward five years, five long uneventful years ... What the hell happened? I was playing semi-pro ball for my hometown team in a lower division and getting paid peanuts, hence the mop and bucket. Every day was the same as the last; my life was nothing but a damn *Groundhog Day* movie.

I needed to bust my vicious cycle of mediocrity and get a change of scenery. Man, I had to get the fuck out of Dodge.

I wrote my university—Rutgers-Camden, the one I'd enrolled at for a single year in 1977. I submitted an application and asked them to accept me back.

I still have the acceptance letter they sent a couple months later. That, and the airfare ticket I bought for a Continental flight from Tel Aviv to JFK. One-way.

11

A Change of Heart

Was I relieved, going back to college? Hell yeah. But there were no rose petals thrown at my feet, so to speak. Sure, I was happy, and for the next seven years my super-stimulated and ravenous mind ate up every ounce of knowledge. Yet I had to work for a living. I took semesters off getting odd jobs like doing carpentry at a construction company, driving a taxi—my shift was from 6 pm to 6 am, six days a week—even working as a bouncer at a peep show. Not exactly a noble occupation, this one, but I wouldn't call it demeaning either. Besides, beggars can't be choosers. What can I tell you? That job definitely had its perks ... Anyway, working and studying was so exhausting that I barely graduated. Still, after tucking those two diplomas into my briefcase, I thought my next move would be to get a teaching job while working on my PhD. I ended up at a bit of a crossroads. My colleagues all seemed more studious and intelligent than me. Plus I was near the bottom of the academic pile. I went through the motions and sent some resumes, but naturally there were no available jobs. It took a little time for me to accept what I was already starting to feel: something about staying in academia didn't sit right with me. I thought to myself, "Is this what I want, living in an ivory tower? Teaching students what my teachers already taught me, and their teachers' teachers, and so forth?" What I wanted was ... well, something more, something different, exciting, better ...

I took the road less traveled. Shoot, I didn't know exactly where I was going next, but at least I moved on with no regrets. *Au revoir*, then, academia! I ditched my Dockers, my pipe and my scraggly beard for a pair of jeans, a leather jacket, a carton of Marlboros and a past-due bill on my rent. I thought I was free as a bird, but while I was mowing lawns for a landscaping company, I constantly wondered, "Now what?" Then luck struck, pretty much out of nowhere: I got a desk job as a Customer Service Rep for an armored truck company called *Brink's*, headquartered in Manhattan. The money wasn't that good, and logistics ... Well, it wasn't sexy, but at least I could stay above water financially.

But I had to laugh. There I was, packing my bags for the corporate world. I even shot over to the flea market in West Philly, where I lived, because it was time to buy a suit and tie! I know, whoever said that money can't buy happiness simply didn't know where to go shopping. But let me go on. You just can't wait for a happy ending, right? I mean my career, not the one in some seedy peep show ...

My career took off like a rocket. I suppose I just happened to be in the right place at the right time. The promotions and relocations I went through were mind-bogglingly swift: I went from a Customer Service Rep to Chief Executive Officer in two decades. I'm not sure where to point the finger at for my success, but there were some critical leadership factors that put me ahead of the curve. I wasn't the smartest man in the room by any means, but I stuck with my mantra, which was simple: if you have the right vision and investment in human capital, maxing out people's potential, then the bottom line will always take care of itself. I learned how to manage people, making them better breadwinners, better teammates. I was taught that no act of kindness, no matter how small, is never wasted. Yeah, yeah—bring on the violins—but I invested in each individual, one at a time.

The past, however, was the past. My career belonged to *the man I used to be*. It means nothing anymore.

But ... does it really? I asked myself, *is there anything I was grateful for in my entire career?* The answer had to be from within: it's me. Those seeds I planted have grown and blossomed because of me. Through them, I found a second self—whether I realize it or not. That self is shining brightly, and my career was a perfect example. But when Aphasia reared its ugly head, I buried it deep inside of me, surrounded by walls of negativity.

I want to tear down those walls, bringing forth that light, which was there all along. I don't consider aphasia a friend by any means, but it inspired me by doing my damnedest to slowly chip away at my gloom, pouring on positivity. I just need to apply those gifts into our companionship—as inadvertent and unfortunate as it is—for all to see.

PART III

The Light Within

12

Our Own Tree Story

My twenty-seven-year marriage to my wife, Carolyn, was rocky even before my condition. The start of our relationship was wonderful: we lived together in a small, cozy apartment in West Philly. I was finishing up my master's degree; she was an employee for the Philadelphia Museum of Art. We adopted our dog, Marley—a tan-colored mongrel of doubtful pedigree—in 1987. Our free-spirited daughter Ana came into our lives in 1992, and lighthearted Isaac followed three years later.

Ana was two weeks old when we rented a two-story, three-bedroom rowhouse in North Miami Beach. It wasn't a gated community but it still had manicured lawns, landscaped gardens, a shared swimming pool and even a playground. Only a few weeks after we arrived, Hurricane Andrew ripped through South Florida. In homage to the victims, we planted a small, 1-foot tall ficus in our backyard. Some months later we moved again—to Italy this time—and the relocation roller coaster just kept on churning.

Joining the ranks of corporate America was life-changing. I was beyond busy working on my career, so it was Carolyn who raised the kids while dealing with our crazy relocations. Over time we began to drift apart. Heck, we probably looked like a pair of ghosts, impalpable and as out of sync physically as we were becoming emotionally.

Fifteen years after moving to Italy, on a bright Sunday afternoon, I flew back to Miami for a business conference. I rented a car but, before driving to my hotel, decided to swing by my old house. I couldn't believe my eyes: that little plant had grown into a monstrous, magnificent tree, maybe 50 feet high and another 50 feet wide, with twisting branches, a thick trunk and serpentine roots that could lift a sidewalk. The occupants—a young family—were sitting down for lunch on their shaded patio, smiling and waving at their neighbors.

It was Carolyn's patience, love, and understanding that kept me afloat after my stroke. But both she and our kids had to digest this new reality with a gloomy, disoriented Shai at their side. She was busy; I was bereft. We were thinking less and less, forgetting the love we'd shared. The coldness between us had become too much to bear.

A couple of years later, I happened to be flying to Florida again. This time I was visiting my uncle and aunt. It'd be nice to stop by the house again, I figured, just one more time.

The tree was gone. The house's windows were rolled down. The front yard's manicured lawn was now overgrown, neglected. No voice was audible, outside or inside or within me.

There's no loneliness like that of a failed marriage.

Forgive me, kiddos. Leaving home tore me apart. I didn't know when or how I could mend things, but I knew I'd have to someday. My affection, love and devotion to you continues to thrive and flourish, helping me maintain my focus on dark days. I promise I'll make it up to you by being a better dad. Before my aphasia and during, my heart still belongs to you. And in a very important way, I do love your mother like no other.

When you found me, aphasia, you ran the gauntlet. You placed an endless obstacle course in front of me and yet, at the same time, you brought a compromise to my loneliness. Without asking, you led me on a long, strange trip with no clear destination. I knew from that day forward that for better, for worse, for richer, for poorer, in sickness and in health, this dance of ours—this life on the stage—was the real deal.

13

Aphasia, Meet Mom

Three Jewish mothers are sitting on a bench in a park, talking about—what else?—how much their sons love them.

"You know the Chagall painting hanging in my living room?" says Esther. "Arnold bought that for me for my seventy-fifth birthday. What a good boy he is, and how much he loves his mother!"

"You call that love??" chirps Minnie. "C'mon! You know the Mercedes I just got for Mother's Day? That's from Bernie. What a doll!"

"Eh, that's nothing,' Yona says. "You know my son Shai? After attending speech therapy, he goes to his psychiatrist three sessions a week. And what does he talk about the entire time? Me!"

When I got my stroke, my mom—a retired secretary that resembled an Erin Brockovich without a miniskirt, working for a real estate mogul—adopted a new nemesis.

Aphasia.

But first things first. Mom believed in me immensely, from the first day I was born. She looked at that beautiful baby cradled in her arms and dreamt about the opportunities she'd give me. She refused to take anything away from my great dreams, my future and my happiness.

We were close confidantes, brutally honest with each other, sharing things that no one else knew. Like her best friend cheating on her husband. Like her boss flying his mistress over for a weekend in Paris. Like our widowed family member having to sell her body just to get by. You might complain that it was a very one-way street; fair enough. I told her things like my substance abuse slip-ups. Like my love life, which I always managed, somehow, to fuck up.

Love, honesty, and transparency made our relationship special, but she also suffocated me with high expectations, which I resented greatly. "The path to success is to be found in education, a profession, in the suitable company- and not just surviving," I quote from some of her letters she used to write me in the 80's. "Social standing brings prosperity. I don't know how you can physically work for many hours, get home to your family and ... dedicate yourself writing poems. Don't ever be satisfied with mediocrity. I will scrape up penny by penny and send it to you, but don't think that this is altruistic on my part—this is not. It is faith in the righteousness' ways knowing that time for reaping the harvest is imminent."

Well, my harvest was bountiful indeed later, financially. But not psychologically. Eventually we grew distant.

When my mother's husband of fifty-two years—our family's oak tree—passed away, she basically died too. For the last five years of her life there were few smiles and too few friends. She sat on her favorite spot on the sofa in a robe, watching TV, sipping her habitual hot tea with lemon and two spoonfuls of sugar. She didn't eat much and the stove in her small kitchen stayed cold and bare.

The last time I saw her, I took a flight to visit her at our home in Rishon. I figured a two-week stay would be fine, but right from the start things were strained. There I was, sitting at the dining room table with my laptop, working on my speech therapy. And there she was, five steps away, with blank eyes. There were no good vibes and the intimacy, which was the hallmark of our relationship, seemed to have vanished. There was very little to talk about. Just me and her and my dad's framed picture on the bookcase looking down at both of us.

The biggest elephant in the room was my aphasia, which made things difficult. Not only was I a very unhappy man—unemployed, divorced, and depressed—I was a failure, a disappointing son whose proud mother didn't register the fact that his condition was here to stay. One evening, I was washing the dishes after a silent spaghetti Bolognese dinner. I'd done my best to make it dad's way—she'd always loved his recipe. She walked into the kitchen, came right next to me, and gently said, "Shai, what's bothering you? Please tell me. You can achieve great things if you could say to yourself *'I will make it, I will be happy'*. We can beat your aphasia—you'll see."

Mood swings have always been an unfortunate part of my emotional makeup. It's an ongoing process managing them, making adjustments to my irritability and depression—and aphasia walking into my life certainly didn't repair the cracks in the foundation. I wish it was something I knew how to fix.

My frustration, my anger, and my fractured psyche snapped. "If you say one more word, I'm getting on the next plane," I erupted.

My mom's face was ashen. She immediately turned on her heels, turned the TV off, and hurried upstairs to her bedroom.

For the next four days, the tension was unbearably thick in our house. I knew I screwed up, but I didn't have the courage or humility to say so. Pretty soon it was time for me to head back to the U.S., and we hugged without saying goodbye. It was so cold, so detached, and for the next few months our phone calls were even shorter. One day she didn't feel well, so an ambulance rushed her to the hospital. Twenty-four hours later and poof, she was gone.

I remember the last time I saw my dad. It was a year before my stroke, and his chemotherapy hadn't started yet so he was still relatively strong. We'd never been very talkative, he and I. But one day, when my mom and siblings were taking a cafeteria break at the hospital, he sat down on a chair next to me.

"Shai," he said, "I have just one request: take care of Ima."

"I will, Aba," I said to him.

He was discharged on the day I had to fly back to the States, so we drove him home together. He chose doing the Chemo here, instead of at the hospital. Hours later, a taxi honked its horn as I bid my parents goodbye. We were all standing by the steel gate at the end of our slate walkway. He hugged me and then I hugged him back. He was thin as a rail. I slid into the back of the taxi and the driver shifted from Park to Drive and off we went. A few seconds later I looked back and waved; he was still there, too weak to wave but upright, gripping the waist-high metal bars. The taxi took a sharp left and we vroomed away. No turn signal, no brake light, no more.

So you see, I let my mom and her old man down. I couldn't take care of her in the end. I can always lay the blame on aphasia, but only partly. All I can do is try forgiving myself for what I did to mom. The way things turned out is a burden I'll carry for the rest of my life.

But I had to let things go. My mom gave me the gifts of life, love, and perseverance. Why wouldn't I use them? As unbearable as I think her life was for those last five years, the only thing she never gave up on was me. Take that cross off my shoulders, accept and move on. I can't bring Ima back and I can't get rid of my aphasia, so embrace, forgive, and guess what? You'll be a better man for it.

14

Yogi for Hire

Sage & Spirit Yoga Studio presents
Restorative Yoga & Live Music
With Devi & Shai
6:00 p.m.–7:30 p.m.

In Devi & Shai's class, you will experience longer-held poses, bring your body into proper alignment and gain mental clarity. Prepare to be challenged by yoga in a new way, while relaxing to the soothing accompaniment of jazz and flamenco guitar.

Devi, a breast cancer survivor, began her yoga practice in 2012 after many years of daily spiritual and holistic practice. She found yoga to be a wellspring of courage, trust and courage.

Shai is a musician, chef, and devotee of yoga. Some years ago, a traumatic injury pushed him to heal and transform his body and mind. Shai's wordless story is being told through his music, a gift that he loves to share.

You remember the poster I borrowed from a yoga studio after class?

You probably don't, but I'll tell you a little bit about another passion I live for: music. I play spiritually-inspired, gentle and uplifting restorative guitar. In truth, my mood—somewhat melancholic—suited my music even before I met Aphasia. As a child, I was an introvert, a wide-eyed country boy. My first memories were of me walking in a field that stretched beyond horizons, pausing and observing the beauty and intricacy of daisies, poppies and other assorted wildflowers. In our family home there was always classical music playing; I studied accordion in grade school. Either way, I developed the highest sensitivity to beauty, art and nature. My guitar was, and is, an instrument that manifests my curiosity, exploration, intimacy and my longings for another. It's an extension of me—my music expresses what I feel without any need for words.

That fusion of yoga and guitar is a magical, transcendental wonder, but me playing guitar was not a result of my stroke. I played before it happened. A famous musician in Israel—his name is Dani Litani knew my dad and gave me a classical guitar as a Bar Mitzvah gift. I was in love with that instrument but it came a close second to basketball. I just never had the discipline or patience to really master that craft—any craft, for that matter.

I was still strumming along, on and off—well, more off than on—for the next forty-plus years. When Aphasia barged into my life, music simply magnified the quiet storm inside me. I suddenly had too much time on my hands. Naturally, I picked up that ol' guitar. Age, rust and arthritis—I knew that I'd never be as good as I wanted to be. Practicing carried me only so far—as Oscar Wilde said, 'only mediocrities progress'—but that's something I could live with. I remember what the great cellist Pablo Casals wrote in his memoir, *Joys and Sorrows*, about practicing: "It fills me with awareness of the wonder of life, with a feeling of the incredible marvel of being a human being." Amen to that, guru. I still play my ass off every day, then tuck my girls back into their cases when I'm done at night.

Oops, did I say "girls?" Sorry, I have an affinity for naming inanimate things. Without further ado, may I introduce you to Peggy O., Annie, and Rosa—my classical guitars! There are other inert loved ones you should know about—there's Mr. Charlie, my adopted stuffed cat, and of course there's Jerry, my beloved, huggable celebrity doll. What would Deadheads like us do without him?

I feel like you're laughing at me, which is perfectly fine. Actually, humans have a well-established tendency to anthropomorphize things that have human characteristics. Which begs the question: does Aphasia qualify?

It does, for me. Why the hell not? After all, I am Icarus—my waxen wings have melted, just like my speech, comprehension and savings account. At least I have a companion, a mythological predator that switches hats and becomes a benevolent, antagonist repentant.

Cheer up, aphasians. Tell ya what, maybe—just this one time—Peggy and I will play you a lullaby. Unless you'd prefer we put on yoga pants and do downward dog instead.

I thought so.

15

All Together Now

I sit down on a bench in my backyard, looking at the huge trees that encircle me. It was dusk in late September and the sky was bursting with colorful hues.

My mind is muted: my spinning wheels are on pause. I shut my eyes and listen closely. The rustling leaves, the whispering breeze, the echoing of wind chimes softly fading ... the traffic hums in the background, not too loud, not gone quiet. Chirping birds, crickets, and cicadas sing rare and different tunes. I'm so grateful to be alive, to be at peace. My heart and my mind are wide open: every bone and limb aches with awareness, feels, sees, hears and knows the silent voice within me, so true and so clear. What a wonderful life it is when my world—inside and out—is in perfect harmony. I finally belong to myself.

Come on, aphasians, let's celebrate with song! Sing together:

All we are saying is give peace of mind!

(All together now!)

ALL WE ARE SAYING
IS GIVE PEACE OF MIND!

Okay, okay, you get the gist. But let's give it a chance, I say. You see, one consolation of aphasia is that it's relatively easy to just turn off our brains, tuning out the outside world; that way our stressed and overloaded minds can take a well-deserved break. So go ahead and relax, meditate, and enjoy the spiritual connection. If you'd like, come and sit in a sacred gathering at your choosing. Like my favorite—a yoga studio where we worship, chant, play music and sing mantras that offer a path to the divine. I challenge you to put down your figurative canes and crutches and step out of your comfort zone. We still have to battle our own demons, after all—I know I do—but there's something inside of us that's greater than any obstacle. So why not try to see the light in a different, perceptive and blissful way? Even if we claim to be fulfilled, why not venture to some higher, ethereal grounds?

I can hear the grumble, so hold your horses, aphasians. I'm too much of a realist. For me, connecting with my spirituality doesn't necessarily require the presence of any gods or goddesses, deities, wandering souls or pseudo-omnipotent, string-pulling puppet masters. I don't particularly care for astrology, moon celebrations, reiki therapists, fortune-tellers, crystal healers, shaman sorcerers, psychics, priests, rabbis and pop eyes and bye-byes ... I respect it all but it ain't my cup of tea. I'm talking about a pure state of being, uncluttered from anything and everything that might litter our minds and our egos.

That consciousness of ours is a shapeless, boundless, and endless life force, one that lights our world with a million candles that refuse to extinguish. It's a concept that arose unbidden, hard to describe, yet so powerful and awesome that it humbles me to the core. It's not about language or words, meaning or context, but rather an unspoken dialogue that directly connects and merges us with the universe: me with Aphasia, her with you, you with me. The rustling leaves, the whispering breeze, the silent voice, the sense of belonging. All it takes is closing your eyes and donning a smile.

When you wake up, you'll find you're not alone. Look up—there, behind dark clouds, lay hidden the sun.

16

Fare Thee Well

It's already been more than ten years or so since aphasia met my fate.

I had a hell of a ride. I've visited and/or lived on every continent except Australia, which, by the way, is on my bucket list. Yup, *the man I used to be* enjoyed every minute, every mile; but when Aphasia lobbed a grenade into the middle of my life, that desire exploded into pieces. At first, I fought like a wounded lion. I was unemployed, I was losing time, I had nothing to do, but deep down inside my lion heart I knew I needed to find my pride. I needed to get back on my feet financially, mentally, physically and spiritually. This old lion was not ready to give up his roar yet.

I remember booking a flight to Las Vegas to attend the annual jewelry show, where I hoped to reconnect with some old business contacts. I came home empty-handed: some ignored me and others gave excuses for not being able to help me find work. However, some months later, I did get a call from an old friend and colleague who offered me a job. He flew me over to his regional headquarters in Hong Kong, hiring me despite having learned about my condition. That was brave and kind of him and even though that gig didn't last long— Aphasia showed up big-time, perplexing him and his staff, leaving me feeling embarrassed and vulnerable. So we both apologized; he voided my contract, paying me a nice severance. We shook hands and hugged, then off I went flying back home with my tail between .. wait, sounds like déjà vu all over again, doesn't it?

But here's the thing: was I pissed off, hurt, alienated? Absolutely, at first. It took some time for me to pour it all out, literally slamming my fists against the wall. Being permanently stuck with aphasia, I forced myself to re-examine, reboot. If I want to be enlightened—which I desperately did—then know yourself first. I began to let go of the reins on aphasia's runaway chariot and gradually became more accepting and forgiving. Aphasia shut a window on my language, but also opened many other doors— bringing in compassion, humility and kindness. Suddenly an inner world appeared, vast and extraordinary, letting me see things I'd never seen before.

I was done with commercialism and frivolous

excess. Being aphasia-stricken, I brought new items into my personal agenda: simplicity, modesty, minimalism, liberty and spirituality. With my career gone, so too were my Armani business suits, my designed jeans and my polo shirts stitched with crocodiles—which I ceremoniously threw into the nearest Goodwill bin. It was the perfect time to strip from the waist up and get a slew of inspirational tattoos. I sensed that this job in Hong Kong would be the last time I'd be a legitimate executive, so two days before my flight I spent the whole weekend getting inked at a famous tattoo shop in Central—Hong Kong's frenetic business and retail hub. That tattoo gun was buzzing like a thousand bumble bees, a mix of pain, ink and blood. My tattoo artist's name was Sze, which sounds like the letter "C." Her name was very interesting: the top part of that Chinese letter was a field but looked like a brain, and the bottom part meant "heart," so her name suggested "thinking from one's heart."

While designing my skin with that gun, Sze told me about her life. When she was only twenty, she followed her heart and started her tattoo journey. For the next fifteen years she not only established the best tattoo studio in town, but she was also an activist for women's rights, poverty, and many other charitable projects that she created. I looked her up online years later. What a remarkable woman—so giving, so loved.

She passed away a couple of years after tattooing me from breast cancer. Way too young. I wear my broken heart—and her ink—on my sleeves, forever. I'm fully aware that some of us don't have the privilege of surviving our medical challenges.

After my brand-name attire, I ditched cigarettes. You may think it's not easy, but you're wrong: it's the easiest thing ever. I've done it a thousand times! Jokes aside, I have to admit—I've always had a love affair with that curse. It was partly my parents' fault. Tidal waves of sweet nicotine memories, familiar scents in our family car, in our home, on the clothes all us kids wore, a heavenly concoction of cigarette smoke, perfumes, and Turkish coffee—those sensations were ingrained in my brain. There's mom and the clothes she wore in the 60's and 70's, a fusion of cool, mod, hippie and bohemian, flamboyant. Always holding a cigarette, tilting her head slightly sideways, her eyes gazing dreamily. And there's dad shaving with his old-fashioned barber's kit—a brush, a switchblade razor, and a bottle of Aqua Velva—wearing his striped pajama pants and, of course, a cigarette dangling from his mouth. Hell, back then even dogs smoked. That was priceless. I miss them so much. I'm blowing an imaginary smoke ring right now in their honor.

The last ritual I gave up on was my bi-weekly trip to my local salon. After four decades of military and corporate-mandated haircuts, I let my hair grow long. The only other time I visit that fine establishment is when I get a manicure, especially for my right hand. My guitars are beyond grateful to me.

Bottom line? I'm in the process of tearing down those walls—literally and figuratively—and diving head-first into a clear pool of exploration and discovery. Transformation complete? Not quite yet, not ever, I imagine. With my aphasia, I fear nothing. I know that a journey of a thousand miles begins with a single step. I know that Aphasia is not the most welcome guest, or the most popular kid in school, but if society has the vocabulary to understand what victims of stroke are enduring, and know even what aphasia is, then people like myself would not be so isolated in their false shame. We aphasians—or anyone for that matter with disability—are at times trapped in a gated community, but I tell you: the gates are never locked. Please, then, come in or out at your leisure because there is truly nothing to be afraid of. We're grateful for having caregivers and healthcare professionals and family members, and friends. Now is when we need you most. Understandably, people run for the hills and avoid any contact with us, feeling awkward and unsure of what to say or do. It's one thing to lose certain abilities, but it's another to lose your identity, purpose and the people you love. I'm containing aphasia's unkind nature, transforming my inner self for the better, swallowing my pride and my losses—heartbreaking as they've been. I made up my mind to help people understand that our lives can still be close and should always be integrated. We all need to find a way to stay connected, to be unafraid nor feel awkward around someone who has changed.

I finally come to the realization that I've spent enough time around Aphasia to know a goddess when I see one. You know, the gods who sent her—was it Zeus, or whatever—remember? Love, heal, light, all that shit? Well, congrats, aphasian—it fuckin' works! It's Aphasia who taught me how to love myself once more, in a deeper way. The bitterness I had for *the man I used to be* was replaced by the happier, improved and mischievous *me*. Understanding aphasia is about as close to real absolution as one can get. I'm still learning how to go easy on myself and my disability, to poke fun at myself through humor, irony, even sarcasm. I know I constantly stumble and fall, with or without profane epithets, but I find myself grating less, smiling more, laughing at my own expense at my unpredictable life. For the first time in almost a decade after my stroke, I've finally learned how to love, period.

And healing? I'm in the process, as endless as it is, of healing *from* you, Aphasia; yet at the same time, you *are* my healer. Like a nurse that injects a potent vaccine, a healthy dose of gentility and grace, you're saving me from my darker self. Angst and exasperation used to be my specialty; now I get up every morning to face the day with vitality, hope and resolve. It eases my pains, helping me to modify my fractured brain. The last step of healing, I say, is using what happened to me to help others.

And the light? It illuminates the truth within me. Through you, Aphasia, I peeled my onion, shedding layers one by one until I was left buck naked—pure, totally transparent. Through you, I've shucked my fear and insecurity, my self-importance, and my stockpile of vacant aspirations—from career success to monetary rewards. All I had left was my faith in myself. It's your fault, Aphasia, because your truth is a reflection of myself, both lighting my way forward. It was you who made me see how beautiful I am, how blissful we all are, despite our condition.

You already know the lyrics: *'Once in a while you get shown the light / In the strangest of places if you look at it right.'* The catch was "if": if I was courageous enough to unveil my mask—blemishes, scars, and all—and deal with aphasia head-on. It was her mission to get me to tell my story, and I never would have done this without her. And now I want to spread awareness and mindfulness and the word 'APHASIA', waving my flag wide and high.

I ask you then, aphasians—what about you? If you're down on your luck, would you give it a try, too? Our personal hardships rear their ugly heads sometimes, but do not fear. Do not dread asking questions, hard and existential as they may be. Be patient and know that we don't always need to have answers. Every life-altering condition or event changes things. We all have to make sacrifices and adjustments. Everyone has their own particular lists, as I have mine. There are things that we will all miss.

What we all share is the opportunity for renewal, a chance to reinvent ourselves, finding new purpose and intention to live our days connected with ourselves—and therefore with others. Most people deserve a second chance; this is one that you give to yourself. As ol' Jerry always says, *Just keep truckin' on!*

Come on, then: let's open the gates—yes, metaphorically speaking. If we want to advocate for aphasia, then we need to blow the horn, tap the tambourine, and join forces. Our tales aren't done and told—not by a long shot. Let's live, learn, rehab, share, connect and grow.

It's our time to shine!

END

Afterword

From: Ana Anbar
To: Shai Anbar
Sent: Monday, December 5, 2011 10:23 PM
Subject: hi

Mom told me you're having an ablation on tuesday. Just acknowledging that it's happening, there's no need to say "I hope it goes well" or whatever because I know it will. Speedy recovery is best because once I'm home, I'm going to be working out a lot and I need a sidekick...or a hardass to tell me to keep going...

Love you

Sent from my iPhone

From: Shai Anbar
To: Ana Anbar
Sent: Tuesday, December 6, 2011 06:35 AM
Subject: hi

You working out?? That's a first...:-)
I'll be fine baby. Takes much more than this to bring this old man down.

Love you,

Aba

Acknowledgements

Many thanks to the following:

Alex M. Ing, my main editor—your patience and understanding was a life saver. Jessica Schwartz, for your prompt and creative finishing touch. Dani and Sybille, for your insightful commentary. Sharon Glaser—it'll be almost two years ago when you sent that thick manuscript with your insight and tact. Surgery was successful! Chrysa Golashesky, you are something special! National Aphasia Association (NAA), Philadelphia Aphasia Community at Temple (PACT), Aphasia Resource Collaboration Hub (ARCH) and so many inspirational endeavors on social media. Special thanks to Carol Dow and David Dow at Aphasia Recovery Connection (ARC), you are my inspiration! Carolyn, to watch us dance is to hear our hearts speak. Nir Freund, Oded Hadani, Arie Grimberg—distance means so little when true friendship means so much. Shalom Ben-Ami, you're a champ! Niva Kaspi, for assisting me in translating my poetry into English. Tamar

Lipszyc—you're right, books are the real thing! Shelly and Kathie, what a magnificent patchwork quilt in our lives! Ofer and Avi at Malca—I wish I could have made you proud. Lauren and Marcie at Jaipure Yoga, and Kristen at The Yoga Ground for giving me a chance to play my guitar. Kate, Savitri, Andy—my gurus at Montclair Kundalini Yoga—you are my church! *Sat nam!* Edward Tierney, "Buddy", and your brother James "Jim" Tierney—life ain't the same without you. Rest in peace. Andy Culpepper and Eitan Bartal—my girls are your creations. Michael Obel-Omia, for recommending Stillwater River Publications. Dawn and Steven Porter, for all you've done for me getting published.

Suzanne Gili Post, my true one. When I had no wings to fly, you flew to me.

About the Author

Shai Anbar is the author of *Goddess Aphasia*, a hybrid of memoir and creative nonfiction that depicts the arduous journey of a stroke survivor diagnosed with aphasia but with a quirky twist: the personified character of Aphasia herself. As a businessman-turned-aphasia advocate, Shai's sole intention is to raise awareness about aphasia so that it becomes more than just a term in a medical textbook. He's using a platform to shine the light on disability—specifically on aphasia—where resilience and inspiration are not always household names. This novella should be relevant for any reader.

Shai was born in Jerusalem, 1960. He lived and worked in a corporate setting on six continents. Over twenty-plus years' experience, his diverse background ranged from established companies to fledgling secure tech startups. Shai earned a B.A. from Rutgers-Camden University in New Jersey and a Master's in Philosophy from Temple University in Philadelphia, Pennsylvania. He currently resides in Haddonfield, NJ, with his partner, Suzanne.

www.ingramcontent.com/pod-product-compliance
Lightning Source LLC
Chambersburg PA
CBHW060203050426
42446CB00013B/2975